WELLINGBOROUGH MEMORIES

Living up to its name, this is Swanspool on a beautiful summer's day on Tuesday 22 July 1958. *(Northampton Chronicle & Echo)*

WELLINGBOROUGH MEMORIES

Joyce and Maurice Palmer

W. D. WHARTON
WELLINGBOROUGH

First published in 1995 by
W. D. Wharton
37 Sheep Street
Wellingborough
Northamptonshire NN8 1BX

ISBN 0 9518557 5 1

Designed and typeset by John Hardaker, Wollaston, Northamptonshire
Printed and bound in Great Britain by
Butler & Tanner Ltd
Frome, Somerset

ACKNOWLEDGEMENTS

We would like to thank the following for their help in the production of this book:

Robert Wharton, for a large contribution to the photographs and for assistance in writing the captions.

Marjorie Veal, for photographs and postcards from her collection.

Wellingborough Library, for allowing us to select items from the late Mr Lawson Pratt's collection.

Mark Edwards, Editor of the *Northampton Chronicle & Echo*, for permission to use pictures from his paper's archives.

John Darker, for the loan of postcards from his extensive collection.

Richard Coleman, for his assistance in finding additional material.

Mark Higlett, for printing some difficult negatives.

D.L. Photography, Earls Barton, for their assistance.

John Hardaker and Michael Sanders, for their professional expertise in editing and arranging the printing of the book.

Photographs not otherwise attributed are from the authors' collection.

Front end-paper caption
The damage on the east side of the Market Square after one of four bombs hit the shops opposite on Monday, 7 August 1942.
Six people were killed, but as it was a holiday there were, luckily, fewer than usual people about. Patrons of the Regal Cinema, just to the north end of the Square, had a narrow escape.
(*Collection of Mrs E. Pettitt*)

Rear end-paper caption
The destruction of the west side of Market Square on Monday, 7 August 1942. The Hind Hotel can just be seen on the extreme left.
The German Dornier 217 bomber which dropped the bombs had a swift retribution as it was shot down by a Spitfire in open country near Finedon.
(*Collection of Mrs E. Pettitt*)

CONTENTS

Introduction 7

Market Square and Market Hill 8

Market Street 21

Midland Road 38

Cattle Market area 53

Cambridge Street 56

Sheep Street area 62

Zoo Park 84

Croyland Abbey area 101

Silver Street 108

Swanspool and All Hallows 117

London Road to the River Nene 121

Midland Road Railway Station to Finedon Road 135

Gold Street area 148

Broad Green area 155

Oxford Street area 161

Queensway 169

Aerial and rooftop views 174

Wilby area 187

Index 192

Bernard J. Bale, chimney sweep of 49 Havelock Street, caught between jobs in Victoria Road circa 1970 by the camera of Mr A. Viccars. All chimneys were swept with a hand brush and rods, the soot being bagged and carried away on the sweep's bicycle. (*A. Viccars*)

INTRODUCTION

Wellingborough has seen enormous changes in the 50 years since the Second World War. Indeed, so much has changed that not much of the town centre remains from what a demobbed soldier would have returned to in 1945. Traditional local industries – boot and shoe making, the iron works, rail-freight operations and the breweries – have either declined or vanished, and the massive influx of new industries, services and people (particularly from the London area) from the 1960s onward has resulted in a rapid expansion from compact market town to a semi-cosmopolitan community.

On the site of the old gas holders in London Road and beyond to the 'Three Mile Spin' there grew the Denington Estate, the first of several industrial estates which have brought a welcome diversity of employments to Wellingborough. Impetus for this was provided by the then Greater London Council which sponsored the town as a development area for what became known as 'London overspill', and the GLC, in collaboration with the local council, built huge housing estates at the edges of the town to accommodate the migrating London families.

The ever-increasing pressure on the town's facilities from a steadily growing local population eventually led to the building of the Arndale Centre and its associated multi-storey car park. Although at the time offering much greater convenience for shoppers, this major redevelopment was perhaps the point of no return for Wellingborough as known and loved by those born and bred in the town. Old lanes and features vanished forever – and the commercial and aesthetic repercussions are felt as keenly today as when it was built in the mid 1970s.

Also the increase in road traffic, and the resulting one-way systems, have had an inevitable effect on the town's character. But with today's more enlightened view, the Council's provision of car parking and the creation of pedestrianized areas in the town centre, steps in the right direction have been taken.

Along with many other towns, Wellingborough has lost much through over-zealous redevelopment – the 1959 demolition of the old Corn Exchange dating from 1862, afterwards the Regal Cinema, was an early example – but the reprieve of the facade of Hatton Hall, the rescue and restoration of the Tithe Barn, the creation of the Heritage Centre in part of Croyland Hall and latterly the prestigious Castle Theatre and Arts Centre, incorporating the old Market Hall and creating a focal point in the town, reflect a welcome concern for the town's future.

Before the reorganization of local government in 1974, when Wellingborough achieved status as one of the new Boroughs, the town's motto (instead of today's 'Forward Together') was 'Look to the Past to Improve the Future'. Much that we valued and enjoyed is now in the past, and the future has still to make up for those losses. In the meantime we have collected together a special selection of both black-and-white and colour photographs of Wellingborough in the post-war years. These are designed to rekindle memories of our town as it was – not back to Victorian times as in our previous books – but concentrating instead on its changing appearance over the past five decades.

Joyce and Maurice Palmer
1995

The Corn Exchange (Regal Cinema) tower and cupola and All Hallows church photographed from Sheep Street, in the mid-1950s, after removal of the traffic lights and substitution with the one-way road system. The Pagoda on the right was then a bus shelter and meeting-place for disabled ex-servicemen in their special hand-pedalled tricycles.

Compare this scene with the one above. The Regal Cinema was demolished in 1959 – perhaps the first of the town buildings to disappear as part of preparations for town centre redevelopment. The whole range of buildings from the right towards the Market Square were soon to follow, including the Evening Telegraph office (second from right). The Pagoda by this time had become a newsagent's shop. (*John Darker*)

After the end of World War II, Winston Churchill, Britain's wartime hero, was voted out of office and a Labour government was put in power.
Here we see the Prime Minister, Mr Clement Attlee, giving an address outside the Regal Cinema, with
(left) the then MP for Wellingborough, Mr George Lindgren, and (right) Mrs Attlee and the local agent, Mr Cyril Faulkner before the General Election of 1951.

A view from the corner of Sheep Street towards All Hallows church in January 1972. The white building was the Exchange Hotel, formerly the Three Tuns, the name having been altered after the building of the Corn Exchange in 1861-62. (*Robert Wharton*)

The scene from 37 Sheep Street in May 1974.
Note the new Technical College (now Tresham College) in opposition to the Parish Church and the library building in Pebble Lane.
Not-so-old Wellingburians will remember the fire siren (the old wartime siren), on top of the College building, which was used to call out the retained fire crew.
The Flower House restaurant in the foreground used to be James's Corner, later Jessops. (*Robert Wharton*)

The lower Market Square and the Regal cinema in 1958. The building on the left housed the antiques shop of Mr Leslie Dykes, and Gillitt & Gillitt, auctioneers and accountants. (*Lawson Pratt collection*)

PROGRAMME

For JUNE, 1958.

THE REGAL

Wellingborough

Phone 2317
Manager — Cyril W. Desborough

Opening Times :
Sunday Continuous from 5-30
Monday to Friday
Continuous from 5-45
Saturday Continuous from 2-0

Prices of Admission :
STALLS 1/6 and 2/6
CIRCLE 3/3 inc. Tax

One of the last programmes before the cinema's closur

Demolition of the Regal cinema in 1959 looking back at the lower Market Square. Note the projection room windows above the balcony entrance. (*Lawson Pratt collection*)

Market Hill from Market Street. The Fine Fare supermarket replaced the Regal Cinema which had been a notable town landmark for over a hundred years. Many townspeople were sad to see its departure. The only building visible here that has survived the hand of progress is the little kiosk on the left which began life as a shelter for those awaiting horse – then motor – buses, and it became known as 'the Pagoda'. The supermarket building was itself demolished in 1995.

White Place, looking east in January 1973. To the right is the side door of the Exchange Hotel, and further back is the rear entrance of Woolworth's. The store was rebuilt on an enlarged site taking in the old Barclays Bank location next to Pebble Lane, during the town redevelopment in the 1960s and '70s. (*Robert Wharton*)

The rear entrance of Woolworth's, White Place circa 1966. The store incorporated part of the walls of the earlier Pendered's Arcade or Emporium.

White Place in May 1972, looking east towards the lower Market Square (Market Hill). (*Robert Wharton*)

This fine building of ironstone, with bands and dressings of limestone, was part of the business of the Pendered family. Here it is being used as the children's section of the Public Library shortly before demolition. The Exchange Hotel is on the right, and on the left is the egg packing station. The road through the arch leads into White Place.

The east side of Market Hill with the old Manchester and Bradford building, here occupied by Timpson's shoe shop.

Something fascinating must have been 'on offer' on this market stall in the 'swinging sixties'.

In May 1972 The Exchange Hotel stands with its sign removed and empty – the last days of this particular 'watering hole'.
(*Robert Wharton*)

The west side of Market Hill in June 1967. Demolition of the auctioneers Messrs Gillitt and Gillitt's premises. The buildings on the right are in Silver Street. On the gate is an advertisement for Williamsons, house furnishers, of Silver Street, one of Wellingborough's family businesses, sadly no longer trading.

Above: Painted wall sign in White Place in February 1973.
The words 'Pendered & Co., Cabinet Maker & Upholsterer' can just be made out.
(*Robert Wharton*)

Right: Pebble Lane on a market day in 1972. The Library and
new shops had yet to make their debut on the right.

This picture of a market day in 1975, shows the new library building and shops on the right.

Markets have been held in Wellingborough since 1201 (and probably earlier 'unofficially') and they are still a major attraction for shoppers. This is a sunny scene in 1975.

Market Street, with entrance to Pebble Lane in mid-distance with Barclays Bank on the corner and Woolworth's 'old-style' in 1977. The figure in front of the old Boots shop is Mr Lawson Pratt, who was a keen photographer of Wellingborough and whose collection was to be loaned to Wellingborough Library. (*Lawson Pratt collection*)

Finch & Denyer's drapery, Market Street, in February 1973. This was a former town house of the late Georgian period. Most shops were initially opened on the lower floors of ordinary dwellings in the town, the owners moving their living quarters to the rear and upper parts of the buildings. Woolworth's can just be seen at the far right and to the left is Morris Smith the jeweller – a situation little changed today. (*Robert Wharton*)

April 1974. Timpson's shoes now occupies Finch & Denyer's shop (they had moved from the bottom corner of Market Hill, as in a previous picture). Leases and rentals became short as time for redevelopment approached. Morris Smith moved temporarily into the narrow part of Market Street, later returning to a new shop, more or less on the old site. (*Robert Wharton*)

Pebble Lane, looking towards Market Street, in about 1962. Houses at the near end had been demolished at the beginning of a pre-war programme of slum clearance/redevelopment which was halted by the war.
The shop was formerly a pawnbrokers ('Uncle's'), and in its last years was a toy shop 'Tawtoys'. (*Robert Wharton*)

Pebble Lane from the south in February 1973 when it was an attractive walk-through. (*Robert Wharton*)

The Salvation Army Band in Market Street (in about 1950). At the left is The Crown inn and Green & Valentine, drapers and milliners, with 'the Pagoda' bus shelter in the foreground. Note the traffic lights which were first installed in 1938. (*Lawson Pratt collection*)

The lower corner of the Market Square and Market Street in 1977, showing the complete row of shops up to Pebble Lane – Timpson shoes; Express Cleaners; H. Morris-Smith, jewellers; Finch & Denyer, drapers; Woolworth & Co. Ltd; Barclays Bank. (*Lawson Pratt collection*)

Market Street, circa 1964, with the Hind Hotel in the far distance. On the left is Dixon & Parker, men's wear, with the Cosy Café above it, and Boots the Chemists on the right. Just visible near the van is the site clearance for a new Anglia Building Society's office.

In the mid-1960s a Tesco store was built on the south side of Market Street, but by August 1974 it was gone – see below. A new Tesco later opened in the indoor shopping centre. The gap here was later filled again by new premises for the National Westminster Bank. *(Robert Wharton)*

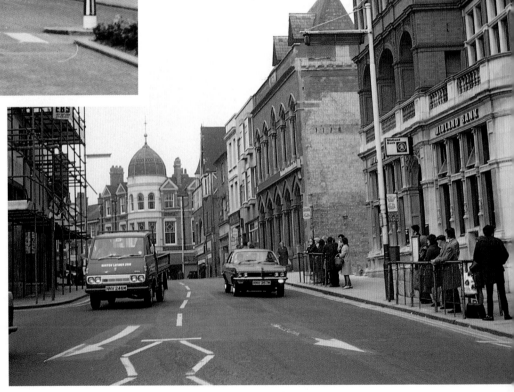

Market Street in April 1974. The Anglia building, newly inserted, next to the Evening Telegraph office which had moved from Market Hill. The Co-operative menswear shop on the corner of Cheese Lane is now empty. (*Robert Wharton*)

Another view of the buildings above from the opposite direction. (*Robert Wharton*)

Market Street seen from the Granville corner in about 1950. This was well before the advent of yellow lines. Instead a solitary and more sedate circular 'No Waiting 9–5' sign proclaims the parking restrictions. *(John Darker)*

A wet Market Street on Tuesday, 5 September 1961.
The lady striding across the road under the Boots sign is Mrs José Marsh, the wife of William E. Marsh, the former brewer at Campbell Praed in Sheep Street.
Mrs Marsh ran a dancing school in the town. *(Northampton Chronicle & Echo)*

Dixon & Parker's corner from Midland Road (also in May 1974). Jessop's tool shop was a mecca for 'do-it-yourself' old-style – they also sold radios and electrical items. The shop was to move (three times) to other premises during the redevelopment in the town. Next door is part of the first of the long run of Co-operative shops. Many Wellingburians deeply regret the passing of such shops and the individuality of the various styles of architecture which made up the character of the central area. (*Robert Wharton*)

Dixon & Parker's menswear shop seen from Market Street in May 1974. The Cosy Café sign has gone. This corner of Midland Road became part of the town centre redevelopment scheme and is now a travel shop.

Now converted into a shop, this building was the Old Kings Arms public house, facing Midland Road (May 1972) and its name is still visible. Like the Exchange Hotel, it was allowed extra opening hours on market days under the old licensing system. (*Robert Wharton*)

Market Street looking towards Gloucester Place in the 1950s. Messrs Pearks was a long-established chain of provision stores which later became Liptons. On the right is the Granville's cake and confectionery shop.

Market Street in the late 1940s. Two-way traffic and the Rover car dates this just after the war. The bus must be coming soon! (*Wharton collection*)

Market Street around 1950 looking towards the Hind Hotel.
The Crown Inn, between Lloyds Bank and Green & Valentines's shop, belonged to Praeds Brewery in Sheep Street. (*John Darker*)

Another 1950 view of Market Street at the junction with Whitehorse Yard which led to the car park which used to adjoin the market, now occupied by the Public Library. All the shops on the left have since been refurbished to retain their individual architectural styles. *(John Darker)*

Market Street and Midland Road corner in the early fifties. A quiet day, most likely a Sunday. The Granville opened around 1900 as a temperance hotel. *(John Darker)*

Market Street and Gloucester Place in about 1962, with The Globe inn on the right, Saxby Brothers
pie and provision store at far left and Mence Smith's hardware shop.

An April 1974 view of Midland Road, with part of the Lyric cinema complex to the left. The street has a decidedly melancholy air. (*Robert Wharton*)

A later view of Midland Road, west side, in 1974. This would have been the last corner-shop 'sale' before demolition.
(*Robert Wharton*)

Some of the Co-operative Society shops, closed ready for demolition. The white frontage once gave admittance to the coal office and the collecting-point for dividends on shares held by members of the public. On the week previous to 'Divi Day' members collected a warrant which announced the amount to be returned for each £1 spent during the period. Happy days!
(*Robert Wharton*)

In this view of Midland Road the eye appreciates the varied skyline and comprehensive shopping
which continues down to the Lyric cinema at the far end.
Today things have become 'inside out', with the Swansgate centre presenting a characterless cold shoulder
to what was once an attractive and busy shopping area, whilst shopping is now away from view
in what is, admittedly, a traffic-free and weatherless environment. (*John Darker*)

A view of Midland Road looking up towards Market Street on a quiet day in the mid-to late fifties. By the time the buildings on the left were demolished for the new shopping centre, almost all were Co-operative shops. (*John Darker*)

Midland Road with the former Lyric cinema on the left, and the new GPO building looming in the background.
The shop in the centre is Mobile Radio's record shop.
The closure of shops on the west side, when the Arndale Centre was built, had a decided impact on other businesses in Midland Road.

This was the scene in February 1973 at White & Co. just below the Lyric cinema building. The family, father and son, were monumental stonemasons responsible for many graveyard headstones and figures etc. Behind was Ellis & Everard's yard. (*Robert Wharton*)

Another 1973 view of White's stonemasons yard. This and other buildings were cleared for the approaches to the new Commercial Way and the multi-storey car park.

(*Robert Wharton*)

Lower Midland Road shops at the entrance to Glen Bank in 1969. This has remained virtually intact. The crane is at work on the then new GPO telephone exchange building.

(*Lawson Pratt collection*)

Shops beyond the entrance to Glenbank in Midland Road in 1965. The picture shows how the original terrace of stone-built houses had flat-roofed extensions added to form shop frontages. The photographic studio and shop of N.G. Woodhead was patronized by a great number of Wellingburians, especially during the 1920s and 1930s for wedding photographs and portraits. Many people will remember the backdrops and sets, as well as the furniture used in the studio.

Midland Road showing Woodheads and Copes shops in the early 1950s. In the left foreground is the stonemason's yard of White & Co. The entrance to the Lyric Cinema car park is next. There used to be petrol pumps on the dividing island. Woodheads, the photographers, here occupy the same premises as the first studio photographer in Wellingborough – Thomas Miller, who set up some time in the 1860s. (*John Darker*)

Shops in Midland Road from the Lyric cinema to Market Street in May 1974. What was one of the busiest shopping streets of the town has become almost deserted. The building with the clock will be remembered by many people as Archie Kauffman's fashion shop, which had an 'island' window in the centre of the frontage – the blocked entrances at either side can still be detected in this picture. (*Robert Wharton*)

Wellingborough Carnival parade in the late 1960s, taken from outside the police station in Midland Road.

A steam lorry entered in the annual Carnival parade by Phipps Brewery Co., who maintained it for special events and rallies as an advertisement, in Midland Road c. 1967.

Left: An unusual view from Commercial Lane to Market Street, showing Timpson's shoe shop which had moved temporarily to the corner of Market Hill from Finch & Denyer's old shop. This 'gap' was occupied for less than 10 years by a Tesco supermarket.

Right: Looking north in Cheese Lane, in 1974, and demolition is in progress ready for the new shopping Centre. The back of the Lyric Cinema is on the right and the Co-operative offices can be seen in the distance.

Midland Road shops in course of demolition. There were no buildings here until after the railway reached the eastern end of Wellingborough around 1860 and the station was built a year or two later. Previously a wall had run along that area of Market Street, and this was breached in order to give access to the station by the building of Midland Road. It became a travellers' highway and shops subsequently sprang up.

Demolition begins for the new shopping centre – Cheese Lane entrance and Dixon & Parker's corner, with Midland Road and the Post Office beyond.   (*Lawson Pratt collection*)

The Lyric Cinema in Midland Road spent its last years as a bingo hall. The shop on the left was for many years 'Bebe' the ladies hairdresser. The building stands silently awaiting demolition – a fate which had already befallen the shops further up the road.

A side view of The Lyric from Midland Road, during the 1974 clearance, showing what a large building it was. It was the only purpose-built cinema in the town, and initially staged pantomimes and shows on the large stage. It had a large foyer and a wide sweeping staircase to the upper floor where there was a restaurant as well as a large foyer to the balcony seats.

THE JULY 1968 CARNIVAL PARADE
Three photographs taken from the doorway of Jessop's shop near the top of Midland Road.

Above left: The Carnival Queen, Miss Anita Reynolds, with her attendants, on the decorated lorry of A. Lilley. (*Ted Arnold*)

Above: A Carnival band counter-marches past Burtons. (*Ted Arnold*)

Left: The amazing double-fronted Mini, which was seen in many local carnivals, advertising Abington Autovue. A sunny day and the usual enthusiastic Wellingborough carnival crowd. (*Ted Arnold*)

Lower Midland Road between All Saints Church and Castle Street about 1970.
T.M. Hobley & Sons, seed and bulb merchants, with the photographic studio of Eric Timms above the shop.

The Cattle Market off Castle Road in Brook Orchard in 1969. It was opened in 1905, having moved down from the old site where the general markets are held today. The move enabled the market hall and accompanying offices and buildings to be laid out for what was formerly a very busy market, especially for cattle, sheep and some pigs. The buildings are now incorporated into the new Castle Arts Centre, an inspired planning decision to retain and use these notable buildings.

(*Marjorie Veal*)

Castle Road in 1969, with cemetery (London Road) on the right, and Cattle Market buildings. The weighbridge was just in front of the house with the gables. The very apt weather vane has as a motif a cow jumping over the moon. (*Marjorie Veal*)

A motor cycle training scheme session in progress at the Cattle Market on a Sunday morning in 1966. The author was one of those running the scheme (fourth from left).

The RAC/ACV test of proficiency at the Cattle Market on Sunday, 23 June 1963. Left to right: E.F. McIntyre (pupil), B. Bigley (instructor), A.J. Allen (pupil), M.L. Palmer (instructor), Miss H. Pentelow (pupil). The machine is a BSA Bantam 125cc. The pupils used their own machines for learning, but the Wellingborough Motor Club had a 125cc James two-stroke for pupils without a motorcycle. This James came from the Auto-Cycle Union, co-sponsor of the scheme with the RAC. All the instructors were members of the Club, with assistance from a superintendent of the RAC and members of the local police. (*Evening Telegraph*)

Near the Cattle Market is Castle Lane (otherwise known as 'Dulleys Baths'), and the factory of Messrs George Cox, known properly as 'Castle Works', with offices nearest the camera (1983).

'Dulleys Baths' explained. The old sign, date and entrance to Wellingborough's first swimming bath (which closed in 1918 when the pool was covered over to become George Cox's boot factory), within the Castle Works complex (1983).

Members of the Scottish Committee of 100 walking from Glasgow to London, protesting against Polaris bases, march through Cannon Street on their way to Doddington on Thursday, 29 August 1963. The Co-operative Society building on the left is typical of the 'decorated' style of the Co-op's architecture locally.
(*Northampton Chronicle & Echo*)

An early fifties view of Cambridge Street.
There has been little change to the buildings this end of the street, although the shops have all changed hands, some several times.
The Cambridge Hotel, behind the bollards on the right, is now the Leather Bottle pub.
(*John Darker*)

Cambridge Street, north side. Barwick's, a former ladies' and children's clothes shop. Miss Annie Barwick was a well-known figure in musical circles and used to give piano lessons behind the shop, which remained gas lit until it closed in the 1960s. The building has since been renovated. Adkins cycle shop is another well-known local family business.

Cambridge Street in about 1964. The Chequers (left) was then served by the Phipps Brewery
of Northampton, which had absorbed the local brewery of Praed and Co., Sheep Street.
In the far distance is The Rising Sun inn, with The Dewdrop on the right.
The buildings remain comparatively unaltered, although there were formerly at least 10 public houses in Cambridge Street and Gloucester Place.

Looking up Park Road from Gloucester Place. The film showing at The Palace is 'That Certain Feeling', released in 1956 and starring Bob Hope and Eva Marie Saint. This part of Park Road was dominated by Dexters store on the right, a very well stocked tool and hardware shop. They also had a china shop in Midland Road near the Post Office. (*John Darker*)

Park Road looking south after the closure of Dexters' shop circa 1965. 'Get it at Dexters.'

It is interesting to compare this view of Cambridge Street, around 1962, with that on page 57. Many of the shops have changed hands, and one-way traffic is in operation.

The Golden Lion inn seen through the lovely iron gateway to Swanspool Gardens in 1971. This is one of the town's most ancient and historic buildings, being a late mediaeval hall house erected by the Roane family. The escutcheon on the overthrow of the iron gate still had the old town arms on it at this time, including 'the five wells of Wellingborough'. The arms changed somewhat after the town became a new Borough during the reorganization of local government in 1974.

A general view of lower Sheep Street in about 1970. The old office for Praed's brewery (with the clock) is still to be seen, but the Bee's Wing public house and yard have gone, affording an entrance into Tithe Barn Road. Long-established businesses which have now gone include, at the bottom of Sheep Street, Sharp's Grocery Stores and Biggs Shoe Repairers.

The east side of lower Sheep Street in 1972. On the left are a shop and buildings which were pulled down when Commercial Way was built.

May 1974. Buildings in the far left of the picture stand empty prior to demolition. The shop was for many years a sweet shop known as Moon's, and many people in the town will remember Gladys Moon. Lack's flower shop moved a few doors down the hill, whilst the *Chronicle & Echo* office eventually found a home amongst the new shops in Pebble Lane. (*Robert Wharton*)

Sheep Street on Tuesday 5 September 1961. The large shop of J. Horden & Son was to cease trading in that decade. They competed with Wharton's opposite for sales of books and postcards, but it is as a toyshop that they are fondly remembered and have never been replaced in the town. Their display of Hornby trains in the top window at Christmas time brightened many a boy's eyes. In its latter years it was owned by Osborne's (from Rushden) and Mr Horden ran the Silver Record Centre in the old Silver Cinema premises in Silver Street. *(Northampton Chronicle & Echo)*

Sheep Street from the Golden Lion on 5 September 1961. Resurfacing work is in progress, and two constables control what little traffic there is. The Golden Lion was built as a house in 1540. It was known to be the residence of Thomas Roane, a Yeoman farmer in the seventeenth century. He died in 1676 according to monuments in the Parish Church to the Roane family. Later the home of Mr G. Wilkin, printer and artist, it became an inn circa 1830. Reference to Whellan's and Kelly directories shows Jane Oliver as proprietress in 1860. (*Northampton Chronicle & Echo*)

Sheep Street from Doddington Road corner in May 1974. This view will never be the same again. The Swansgate Centre which now towers over the houses makes this Wellingborough's worst aspect. It is ironic that the Council staff see this every day from Swanspool. (*Robert Wharton*)

In place of the brewery 'clock office', a framework of girders heralds a new office block, sadly out of keeping with the Tudor House.

Looking at the car park on the site of the former brewery from the demolition area near the Tudor houses, Sheep Street, where the 'clock office' stood alongside the Bee's Wing public house. All Saints Church is in the distance.

The brewery house/offices during demolition, with Commercial Lane entrance beyond. This building had latterly served as a temporary office for the Co-operative Permanent Building Society (which eventually merged into the Nationwide Building Society) whilst its Thrift House premises in Oxford Street were being redeveloped. The building of the Arndale Centre (later Swansgate) caused great destruction in Sheep Street as well as Midland Road and the area in between, including the old brewery site, factories and some houses in Commercial and Pebble Lanes.

Sheep Street around 1952. The small hatch under the bottom left-hand window of the Hind Hotel led directly to the cellar. The girls pushing their cycles are from the High School in London Road, wearing their summer uniform. *(John Darker)*

Sheep Street in the 1950s.
To the left is the Tudor House restaurant, with the brewery 'clock' office and Bee's Wing pub beyond.
The clock was saved and is now on Randles China Shop in Burystead Place.
On the right is the old brewery house (which came to be used as offices) and entrance to Praed's brewery.

Above: Another view of the car park in 1974 from Commercial Lane.
The multi-storey car park overlies much of the site today. (*Robert Wharton*)

Right: Fire escape to the rear of the cinema, opposite
Cedar Lawn, the brewer's house. The gate on the right
was the pedestrian access from Commercial Lane to
Midland Road. (*Derrick Humphries*)

Sheep Street from Burystead Place in about 1975, with the Hind Hotel on the right.

The bookshop of W.D. Wharton, Sheep Street, in February 1973. The family business began in lower Silver Street in the Victorian era. (*Robert Wharton*)

Looking from the grassed area of Market Square (the aftermath of a World War II bomb which fell behind Halfords in August 1942). Halfords didn't return to Wellingborough. Across the road Green & Valentine Ltd, the large millinery shop, lasted until April 1977. Before 1900 their shop was also in Sheep Street in the block occupied by J. Horden & Son. *(Northampton Chronicle & Echo)*

Sheep Street in the early 1950s, with Horden's toy shop on the left and Praed & Co's brewery further down.
The building beyond Hordens, occupied by Messrs Robinson & Riddey Ltd and G. Smeathers, pastry cook and confectioner, was
soon to be demolished and replaced by the present two-storey building. On the right is the Hind Hotel, and beyond that, Whartons Bookshop.

Looking up Commercial Lane from Sheep Street after demolition of the brewery buildings which were on the right of the picture.

In summer 1974, the buildings in Commerical Lane were being vacated prior to destruction. The empty shop was for many years Mr Hunter's – watch and clock repairer – who closed his shop in 1970 at the age of 86. It was demolished to provide the escalator entrance to the Swansgate Centre.
(Robert Wharton)

Cheese Lane looking towards the town in about 1972, from the junction with Commercial Lane. Mid-left is the Gas Company office and, in the distance, Wellingborough Industrial Co-operative Society offices – its title when an independent body.

Cheese Lane, February 1973, from Market Street. Almost all the cottages were empty. The Gas Company office stands beyond them. (*Robert Wharton*)

Old houses in Sheep Street soon after the end of World War II, looking up to the bomb-damaged properties in Market Street with corrugated roofs, and beyond them the Corn Exchange.
(Wharton collection)

Buildings scheduled for demolition, Commercial Lane. Some areas were perhaps overdue for clearance.

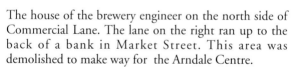

The house of the brewery engineer on the north side of Commercial Lane. The lane on the right ran up to the back of a bank in Market Street. This area was demolished to make way for the Arndale Centre.

Praed & Company's mineral water factory, Commercial Lane. Far left, the garden wall of the engineer's house. Far right, the rear of the Lyric Cinema/Bingo Hall.

Spring 1974, Praed's mineral water factory under demolition.
(*Robert Wharton*)

Cheese Lane, with the Co-operative Society offices sporting the WICS logo above the top windows in May 1972.

(Robert Wharton)

The great increase in population during the period from the mid-1960s gave the Council the idea that a modern complex of shops was needed in the town centre where a good deal of the land was already Council property. A private company was therefore given the contract to build in April 1974, and the Arndale Centre opened for business in June 1977. This picture of Spring Lane in the Centre was taken in February 1978, three months after the official opening by HRH the Duke of Gloucester. On the left is the fountain with its flying swans, which was perversely taken out when the centre's name was changed to Swansgate following refurbishment a decade later.

Cheese Lane cottages looking towards Market Street in 1972/73.
Note the small gated entrance – the only approach to the rear of the houses.

The row of toilets, just inside the entrance gateway, at
Cheese Lane cottages – quite a walk from the cottage
nearest to Market Street! Part of the Gas Company office
can been seen above the wall (1974).

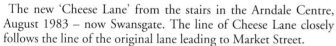

The new 'Cheese Lane' from the stairs in the Arndale Centre, August 1983 – now Swansgate. The line of Cheese Lane closely follows the line of the original lane leading to Market Street.

The old office buildings and tower of Dulley's Brewery seen from London Road in 1974. This firm originated in the mid-nineteenth century and took the swan as its emblem from 'Swanspool House'. Dulley's was taken over and amalgamated with Messrs Campbell Praed & Co. Ltd the brewery neighbour in Sheep Street in 1920. During the second world war the remaining buildings were used by the local Home Guard company as their HQ. One of its members was killed in August 1942 whilst on guard duty when a bomb demolished the main building. (*Derrick Humphries*)

The swan motif on the old clock tower on Dulley's brewery buildings behind 20 Sheep Street in 1974. 20 Sheep Street was once the home of William Dulley, the brewer. This swan, built of brick, was carefully removed from here and mounted in the central square of the new shopping centre as a focal point. Unfortunately, both it and the plaque unveiled by HRH Duke of Gloucester at the opening of the centre were boarded over when the café opened under the stairs in the Swansgate. We can imagine the headlines when they are 'discovered' in some future refurbishment. (*Derrick Humphries*)

Looking towards Sheep Street in April 1974. The Farmers Union (NFU) offices in course of erection in Tithe Barn Road in the background. (*Robert Wharton*)

A view in about 1968 of upper Sheep Street up from the Commercial Lane entrance.

Lower Sheep Street in about 1951, with entrance to the Zoo Park at right.

Zoo Park entrance and Tudor Restaurant with the brewery car park happily opposite. The yard gates below the Zoo Park have been replaced by a single-storey shop building. (*Robert Wharton*)

Zoo Park entrance and old houses, Sheep Street soon after it first opened in 1943, before the wrought-iron gates were installed.

(Wharton collection)

It must seem strange to those who never queued by the goldfish pond to buy a ticket, that there should have been a zoo park so close to the centre of the town. In the 1950s and 60s any Wellingborough family with children visiting would have to go to see the baby elephant, giant tortoise shell, penguins in the pool and the chimps' tea party, not to mention the paddling pool and playground. Economic pressures caused its closure, but the site is still largely intact, although blighted by the Council Treasurer's building. *(John Darker)*

The Zoo was a great attraction for many people, and it became known over a wide area. In the foreground is the extension area which accommodated peacocks (including white peacocks), a llama enclosure and other animals. *(Robert Wharton)*

The Zoo Park with Croyland Abbey in the background. On the lawn in front of the Abbey were held chimps' tea parties. After the zoo closed the Abbey was neglected and became vandalized, but it has since been restored as the Council's Planning Department.
(*John Darker*)

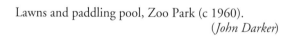

Lawns and paddling pool, Zoo Park (c 1960).
(*John Darker*)

Wellingborough Zoo Park in 1956. Founded on land below Croyland Abbey on part of the ancient manor of Croyland, which land was given by the King to the Abbot of Croyland (now Crowland) in Lincolnshire in the tenth century, the park was opened in 1943 by Mr H. Stevens, who for many years had been the proprietor of a pet shop in Midland Road. The entrance was in Sheep Street, next to the Tudor houses, where the gate pillars can still be seen.

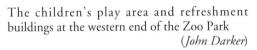

The children's play area and refreshment buildings at the western end of the Zoo Park
(*John Darker*)

A view of the play area from the west side of Swanspool brook, circa 1967. (*Robert Wharton*)

A different picture of the play area, on a cool day from the dress of the people in view (circa 1951) (*Wharton collection*)

Part of the extension to the Zoo Park, which was opened in 1956-57 by TV personality and naturalist, George Cansdale. This allowed use of the Swanspool brook for water birds, such as black swans.

Blondie (christened thus by George Cansdale) was a great favourite at the Zoo Park.

Croyland Abbey in 1968 when the Such sisters were proprietors of the Zoo Park. The private garden to the house was on different levels, with lawns, steps and flower beds. An interesting feature was an enormous ball on a pedestal, made from a silvered materials (like a 'witch's ball') that reflected the scene and the sun. The great cistern, as large as a swimming bath, known as Monks Well was behind the bushes on the left – a rather mysterious and hidden feature.

Terracotta heads set into a wall in the garden below Croyland Abbey (1968). They would seem to represent, from left to right, an abbot, a queen, a monk and a king. The costume suggests the period when the Manor was given to the Abbot of Croyland (now Crowland) in Lincolnshire. Whatever happened to these little works of art?

The Monks' Well in 1968 in Croyland Abbey garden. The cistern was fed by the waters of a spring, and itself watered the Zoo Park below it.

This quaint feature, photographed in 1968, was perhaps an ancient well-head. It was situated close to Monks' Well and let partly into the cistern wall.

On Saturday 13 April 1957 the Zoo Park was open in time for Easter, and this is the Head-keeper Maurice Sharp with Solomon the Lion, aged 5^1/$_2$. Solomon had been born at Wellingborough Zoo and had just returned after three years with Bertram Mills Circus. (*Northampton Chronicle & Echo*)

Saturday 13 April 1957 on the slide in the Zoo Park. Does anyone recognize themself? (*Northampton Chronicle & Echo*)

Amongst all the exotic animals to be seen in the Zoo, swans still have their fair share of attention on 13 April 1957. (*Northampton Chronicle & Echo*)

The Zoo Park in April 1957, showing how it used Swanspool Brook to good advantage. (*Northampton Chronicle & Echo*)

Probably the most popular resident in the Zoo Park – the baby elephant – in June 1962. (*Northampton Chronicle & Echo*)

Looking from inside towards the Zoo Park entrance in Sheep Street in August 1972 about two years after closure. (*Robert Wharton*)

Croyland Abbey glimpsed across the overgrown gardens in 1972. (*Robert Wharton*)

The countryside comes to town. The Swanspool brook in the former Zoo Park as it looked in summer 1972. (*Robert Wharton*)

A 1972 view of part of the Zoo extension area, looking south across Swanspool Brook. (*Robert Wharton*)

The Tithe Barn Road area around 1962 with the barn to Burystead Farm on the right and the rear of the Hind Hotel on the left of the picture.

The National Farmers Union headquarters building under construction on the Burystead site. This must be the most misplaced structure in Wellingborough, being in the centre of beautiful gardens and carefully restored old buildings. How did it happen?

The Tithe Barn before it became part of the redevelopment scheme in the town. Concern over the condition of the early fifteenth-century building, after it had been acquired by the then Urban District Council, resulted in funds being raised and plans being made to assure its future.

Old barn near Burystead Place, 1972.   (*Robert Wharton*)

Buildings facing the Tithe Barn, taken from Burystead Place in 1972. The corner building survived a fire in the early nineteenth century, was rebuilt in 1846 and again in 1975 and is now Randles china shop. The building behind became the Tithe Barn Restaurant.   (*Robert Wharton*)

Croyland Abbey from Burystead Place, with the last remnants of Burystead Farm barn, in 1972. (*Robert Wharton*)

Burystead Place and the Hind Hotel from what is now the Tithe Barn Green area in the summer of 1972.
(*Robert Wharton*)

The Tithe Barn under renovation. In the 1960s the barn was surveyed, and it was agreed that £4,500 would need to be found for restoration work. A Tithe Barn Trust and Committee was formed as a fund-raising body. The interest of Sir Giles Isham of Lamport Hall was attracted and he became a very active promoter, along with Lady Lavinia. In the foreground is the newly laid out Sharman Road car park, and in the background can be seen the Tithe Barn Restaurant building before renovation. (*Marjorie Veal*)

Inside the Hind Hotel in summer 1970. A gathering of the Whitworth family, formerly lords of Earls Barton Manor. The family was celebrating with Earls Barton the millenium of the parish church tower, and also the linking of two sections in the Whitworth family tree, in which the authors of this book became involved. The Palmer (of Earls Barton) family tree indicated the marriages of two Whitworth males with two Palmer sisters at the beginning of the eighteenth century. In the second row, second from the left is the late Brigadier Whitworth. Mr Robin Whitworth, tracer of the family's ancestry, is fourth from the right in the third row. He was aided by daughter Anna (front row, kneeling, with scarf). The former well-known personality, Mrs Dorothy (Sidney) Cook, of 'The Archers' fame, and who used to live in Church Street, can be seen second from the right in the second row. The authors are tucked away at the back.

Buildings around the southern end of the Tithe Barn and the pedestrian entrance to the Sharman Road/Croyland Gardens car park in the summer of 1972. (*Robert Wharton*)

The eastern end of the buildings, with the Adams Insurance building in Burystead Place seen through the trees.
(*Robert Wharton*)

In the early summer of 1972 the Tithe Barn caught fire, to the great consternation of the restoration team. However, the event prompted a reassessment by the Council of the Barn's potential as a town amenity. (*Robert Wharton*)

Another view of the Tithe Barn (the northern end) after the fire in 1972. (*Robert Wharton*)

Silver Street corner with Oxford Street in the early 1950s. The Angel Hotel on the left closed later in the decade – in the last century it was a coaching inn. At this time the Co-operative Society had branches in most areas of the town. (*John Darker*)

Silver Street in the mid-fifties. Notice that parking on the one-way street was on alternate sides. Most of the buildings in view are substantially the same today, but with different tenants. The exception is James's corner, which was demolished and rebuilt as McDonalds. (*John Darker*)

The Flower House Chinese Restaurant in 1973 (now the site of McDonalds). Many older Wellingburians still like to recall the grocery and provision stores on 'James Brothers Corner', when self-service was unheard of, and you could take a chair whilst being served.

The Flower House restaurant, the Mac Shop and Steve Clarke's shoe shop in early 1973.
The building housing the last two businesses was W.D. Wharton's stationery shop with printing works above. When his shop moved to Sheep Street in 1925, the printing works remained until the third storey was demolished following bomb damage in World War II, the corrugated roof being evidence of this until the building was redeveloped. (*Robert Wharton*)

Adjoining the Angel Hotel buildings was the Town Hall, erected in the 1820s. Much business transacted here was later transferred to the Corn Exchange, Market Hill, at the end of the 1860s. All buildings here are now the premises of the Rowlatt family, whose business dates from the eighteenth century – probably the oldest in the town.

Freemans Endowed School at the junction of Silver Street and Oxford Street began life as a free school in the early eighteenth century. A chief benefactor was Mary Roane, whose forebears lived at the Golden Lion in Sheep Street.
The building was demolished soon after this picture was taken, and the school was removed to the old Westfield Boys School building in Westfield Road.

Silver Street, looking towards Sheep Street, in the 1960s. Here we see many long-standing family businesses – Webbs outfitters, Williamson's furnishers, Canty's sports shop, King's jewellers – now all just memories.

Silver Street, west side, in 1963. During the war the Food Office was situated up this ancient lane and around to the right.
(*Marjorie Veal*)

Upper Silver Street in February 1973. The Angel Hotel was once a coaching inn and later a point of departure for horse buses to the railway station in London Road. Note the one-way sign, and Currys shop on the right. (*Robert Wharton*)

Silver Street, Angel Lane entrance, in 1973. The lane is a remnant of a number of small alleys and houses which were cleared to make way for the cattle market near All Hallows Church, later the general market. The enamelled metal advertisements for Colman's starch and mustard are reminders of when this was the tea warehouse, grocery and home of the Norman family. This building has now been absorbed into Armsides Chemists. (*Robert Wharton*)

Upper Silver Street, looking towards High Street, in February 1973. In the distance on the left is the Conservative Club, and Leighton House, once the home of John Woolston, an influential town figure and brewer. (*Robert Wharton*)

Church Way in 1973, another ancient lane, once lined by cottages and the old workhouse. (*Robert Wharton*)

The former Liberal Club, seen here in a later guise as the YMCA building, on Oxford Street/High Street corner in 1963. Locals referred to it as 'the YM' or 'YM corner'. The bus stop outside the High Street entrance brought people to the market and shops – and Saturday night dancers to the hall in the rear part of the building. The youth of the town and district lost this mecca, and the building changed its face once more.

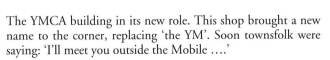

The YMCA building in its new role. This shop brought a new name to the corner, replacing 'the YM'. Soon townsfolk were saying: 'I'll meet you outside the Mobile ....'

A tree planting ceremony in Swanspool Gardens in 1951, a part of the commemoration of the Festival of Britain and to mark the year of office of the Chairman of the WUDC, Councillor E.H. Hearnden (standing left). Mrs Hearnden is holding the spade, and Ian Robbie, Parks Superintendent, is standing by the tree. Amongst the onlookers are Mrs G.H. Cox, Councillor L.R. Higgs, R. Kilby, Borough Engineer, Mr Ralph Ward, solicitor (near dog's head) and Mr and Mrs Harry Sursham of Sursham, Tompkins & Partners, architect (left of the new tree).
(*Lawson Pratt collection*)

The old Grammar School, Church yard, was founded in 1595 and rebuilt in 1620. At far right is the old Technical College building, which had the former Urban District Council chamber on the upper floor when first built. This was demolished to make way for the new College extensions. Part of the newer building (now Tresham College) can just be seen. The picture, therefore, shows 'seats of learning' from the late sixteenth to the twentieth centuries. The old Grammar School is used as All Hallows Parish Hall.

The regilding of All Hallows Church clock in the 1960s. The cast-iron clock face was made at the Wellingborough foundry of William Butlin in 1871, and replaced a wooden dial.

Looking back at the town from the junction of Castle Road and London Road with Swanspool Pavilion on the left. What was the office building of William Dulley's brewery can be seen facing London Road, and the new Technical College building stands high on the skyline.

Swanspool Gardens around 1948 looking over the old croquet lawn. Regrettably, the fine statue of Euterpe (the Greek Muse of music, daughter of Zeus and Mnemosyne) was stolen in the 1950s. This bronze was given to the town by Mr W. Talbot-Brown, architect, in 1932. (*John Darker*)

The top area of Swanspool facing the pavilion, where can be seen the drinking fountain – 'Jotto's fountain' – removed from the lower Market Square circa 1913. The fountain was given to the town by Mr James 'Jotto' Page, Chairman of the Urban District Council, to commemorate the coronation of Edward VII in 1902. It has since been restored, but without its drinking water, and now stands just inside the Swanspool gate facing Sheep Street.

The foot of London Road from Swanspool bridge in 1969. The small house was demolished in about 1971.
Nurse Mayall, who lived in it, was a well-known figure in the town for many years. (*Marjorie Veal*)

Nicholson, Sons and Daniels tannery seen from the north across the flooded meadows of the Nene east of London Road bridge in July 1973.

Whitworth's flour mills and London Road bridge in 1964.
The mills were worked by steam power when built in 1886 by John Battams (known as 'JB') Whitworth.

One of the early factories to be built on the Denington Estate in London Road was that of shoe manufacturers Messrs Sudborough & Wood, who had previously had factories in Mill Road and Park Road. The new factory was begun in 1964, and by 1969 it employed about 120 people. The work progressed through the various departments on the open-floor system of management. This is a view across the factory floor towards the clicking department where the windows look out on to Denington Road.

In this part of the Sudborough & Wood factory, the closed uppers are being pulled over the lasts ready for attaching to the soles.

The Rollei building on Denington Industrial Estate in 1974. The company (now no longer on the estate) imported, distributed and repaired cameras.

Sudborough & Wood's closing department, where the sections of the shoe uppers are 'closed' or machined together, with clicking (or cutting out) of uppers taking place at top right, and the shoe room (where products were given a final inspection and boxed) at the top left. The factory was subsequently demolished and replaced by that of another company.

The cast-iron waterwheel of Turnell's Mill in 1984. The building, set up by the Whitworth brothers in 1874, and mill house were demolished a few years previously, but this wheel remains to remind us of how Turnell's Mill Lane got its name.

Turnell's (Wellingborough) Mill in December 1968. Although built only in 1874 by the Whitworth brothers it was just at the time when steam-powered roll-milling was introduced, specifically to process the new imports of hard wheat from America. Therefore, in 1886, Mr J.B. Whitworth built the Victoria Mills and installed the new roll-milling machines, and what became Turnell's Mill finally came to be used for processing animal feedstuffs.

The Nene Bridge and Whitworth's Mills prior to the new road layout and the building of the A45 expressway.

Victoria Mills, Little Irchester, with Nicholson, Sons and Daniels tannery behind the Nene Bridge in 1969.

One of the last narrow boats to work the river as a grain carrier to Victoria Mills (April 1969).

London Road railway station from the station yard in April 1969. The line opened in 1845. It was closed to passengers in May 1964 and to goods traffic between then and 1972. (*Marjorie Veal*)

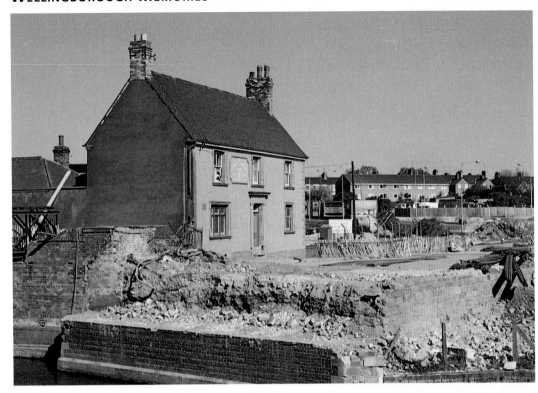

The Crown and Anchor immediately before demolition in 1980.

Remains of the Nene Bridge and the temporary bridge for pedestrians from The Walks in summer 1980. (*Robert Wharton*)

London Road station and Little Irchester from Whitworth's mill on Wednesday 25 May 1960. At the end of the platform and just next to the four vans can be seen the small wagon turntable, one of several that were used in this goods yard to shunt the vans for loading. A line of iron ore wagons awaits a locomotive in the far sidings, and in the far distance towards Wollaston a breath of steam is exhaled by one of the ironstone pit locos. (*Northampton Chronicle & Echo*)

The station, northbound platform, in the early 1960s.

The station looking towards the footbridge at the level crossing in London Road in the early 1960s.

The view from the footbridge in February 1968, with weeds growing on the platforms of the closed station.

The Railway refreshment house from the station footbridge at the level crossing in February 1968. It was built on the site of a former toll-house on the turnpike road system, and was much frequented by tannery and mill workers as well as railwaymen.

London Road station in July 1970 – 'The works of man return anon to nature.'

An 8F class locomotive working a train of box wagons at Mill Road bridge in 1961.

A large party of enthusiasts from the Industrial Railway Society on a farewell tour of the last quarry on 1 October 1966. Iron ore was quarried at No. 6 Pit near Finedon until 1966. The train is seen crossing Finedon Road with loco number 86. The crossing is controlled by a man with a red flag, as was the usual practice.

(Ken Clements – Lawson Pratt collection)

Morris Motors was a major employer in Wellingborough on a site off the Irthlingborough Road with its own siding off the Midland Road Station line. It started as Butlins, with the original foundry – the dark building in the left foreground, and later became British Steel. Morris Motors took over in June 1947, and it closed in September 1981 as British Leyland. The building block on the left is the tractor casting foundry, castings being taken to Bathgate for assembly. On the right is the cylinder head and block casting foundry (castings going to Longbridge for machining and assembly) and in the centre is the fettling shop, with above it the pattern shop. It could well have still been operating had not expansion plans been thwarted by losses by British Leyland from the three-day week during the miners' strike in the 1970s. This site remains a hive of industry as the Laurence-Leyland complex of small industrial units. *(Lawson Pratt collection)*

This shows the relighting of the second furnace in February 1960 at the Wellingborough Iron Co., part of Stewarts & Lloyds. Owing to lack of demand, it had been dormant since 1957. It was lit by an eight-foot long paraffin-doused cotton waste torch, igniting eight tons of firewood and 90 tons of coke, and each furnace was tapped at six-hour intervals, with metal being poured therefore every three hours. On the far left is David Knighton; fourth, fifth and sixth from left are Bill Underwood, Stan Richardson and Jack Gittings. The group on the right, from left to right, are Geof Price, Ralph Hutchings, Arthur Foster and Leo Wozniak.
(*Northampton Chronicle & Echo*)

Blast furnaces at the Finedon Road ironworks under demolition after closure of the works in October 1962. There had been blast furnaces on the site since 1886, when the newly-formed Rixon Iron & Brick Company put their new furnaces into pig-iron production (thus today's Rixon Road). The furnaces changed hands a number of times, and the Stanton Iron Company put new furnaces into blast on the same site in 1933, still using the brand name 'Rixon'.

The Midland Pullman approaching Irthlingborough Road bridge on a wintry day in the early 1960s.

The breaker's yard of J.W. Davies next to the railway on the site of the old brickyard on Friday 17 May 1963. Behind Midland Cottages in Finedon Road can be seen the pipework and chimney of Wellingborough Iron Works. (*Northampton Chronicle & Echo*)

Midland Road station on Monday 12 February 1968 taken from the signal box at the end of platform 2. The footbridge to the far platform has been removed following closure of the Higham Ferrers branch. The coach sidings have been uplifted to enlarge the car park on the right. Steam has given way to diesel hauled trains. (*Northampton Chronicle & Echo*)

Locomotives at work, looking across 'Tipperary' sidings in 1961 from Jubilee Walks. In the foreground is an 0-6-0T shunting engine. Behind Wellingborough North signal box, a Class 8F and Class 9F raise steam. One of the two large locomotive sheds, or roundhouses, can be seen on the left.

A compound 4-4-0 engine on the Leicester train at Wellingborough Midland Road station on 18 June 1955.   (*John Butler*)

A Midland excursion train, headed by a 4F Fowler locomotive, leaving Wellingborough Midland Road station in 1956.   (*John Butler*)

A Fowler 2-6-0 'Crab' heads a freight train through Midland Road station towards Finedon Road bridge on 10 March 1956. This picture was taken from a footpath along the bank above the sidings, known as Jubilee Walks. In the distance is the foundry in Irthlingborough Road. Thomas Butlin set up blast furnaces on the site in 1867, later Wellingborough Iron Company. Between 1947 and closure in the 1970s, Morris Motors (and later British Leyland) used the foundry for engine castings. (*John Butler*)

Beyer-Garratt No. 47969 pulls a 48-wagon iron ore train over the River Nene bridge north of the embankment on the loop from Wellingborough London Road station to the Midland main line on Sunday 26 May 1957. The loop was heavily graded, and continued over the Irthlingborough Road, where the road still narrows for the bridge abutments. It remained open after the closure of the Peterborough to Northampton line for Whitworth's grain shipments until June 1982. (*Ken Fairey*)

Sidings near Finedon Road bridge in 1956. Two 9F Franco-Crosti boilered Standard BR 2-10-0 engines, Nos. 92027 and 92026, are here double-heading a goods train on the down slow line. (*John Butler*)

A view of the Higham Ferrers motor train taken by a passenger on the Northampton train near the Midland station footbridge in 1956. Immediately to the right of the bridge is the railwaymen's lodging house at the far end of Mill Road. (*John Butler*)

Houses in Finedon Road, north side towards the railway, a short time before they were demolished in 1970. Being near to the former furnace complex, these and other houses in the area were much affected by furnace dust which settled on roofs to form a reddish-brown coating. (*Marjorie Veal*)

Work began in late 1960s/early 1970s on the housing development on the north side of Nest Lane – formerly a quiet road which led down to fields, the Ise river and the furnace site. The proposal was that 501 houses be built here as part of an agreement between Wellingborough and London County Council in 1962 and Greater London Council in 1967 which became known as 'overspill'. The project was to house families from the London area in the main. The estate became known as the Hemmingwell Estate after the former farm and well.

Cross Road from Finedon Road in the late 1960s before the development of the Nest Fields area began. Eastfield Park is on the left. (*Marjorie Veal*)

The Pyghtle from Gold Street with the road which led up to the Breezehill School for Girls on the right. The school was later amalgamated with Westfield Road Boys School under the then new policy for comprehensive education and was renamed Sir Christopher Hatton School. The post-war Pyghtle private housing estate covered a former market garden and orchard area. The old right-of-way from Gold Street to Harrowden Road ran through this area on the same line as today's roads, and was much frequented by courting couples.

The St John Street branch of the Co-operative Society's stores, which comprised a grocery and butchery, in 1968. In the distance is the new Technical College building in Church Street.

Sharman Brothers' brush factory, built in 1888, facing along New Street in the early 1960s. The business was begun in 1875 in High Street by W. and A.J. Sharman. The new factory and warehouse employed 30 people at the outset, and was enlarged after a fire in 1912. It became designated for demolition in the late 1960s.

Gold Street in 1968, looking west. The terrace on the right was demolished soon afterwards all the way up to the shop with the sunblind.
(*Marjorie Veal*)

Gold Street – a closer view of the grocers shop with the blind. The building which once adjoined it has left its outline on the side wall of the shop. Gold Street was one of the most ancient areas of the town, but few old buildings of the local stone remain today. The street lost another shop, as can be seen here, when the terrace was pulled down and replaced with a petrol station. Once there were many shops in the area. (*Marjorie Veal*)

Houses in Regent Street, looking towards Havelock Street, in 1969. The buildings were pulled down in 1972 and the area was redeveloped. (*Lawson Pratt collection*)

A pause for a photograph at the Hacksley Brothers yard, date uncertain, in Regent Street. It later became the business of Beeby and Cox.
(*Lawson Pratt collection*)

The houses in Little Park Street were almost empty of people when this picture was taken in 1969. (*Lawson Pratt collection*)

Little Park Street, looking down towards the electricity building in Cannon Street in 1969. (*Lawson Pratt collection*)

The Swan & Nest (now The Cannon) in Cannon Street, from Alma Street, in 1968. (*Lawson Pratt collection*)

Queen Street in 1970. Houses between the Technical College yard and Herriotts Lane. (*Lawson Pratt collection*)

Orchard Terrace at the rear of the west side of High Street from a newspaper photograph. There were a number of houses in yards running off High Street. Some were scheduled for demolition before World War II, but town improvements of this kind had to wait until the post-war period saw plans taken up again. (*Marjorie Veal*)

The New Inn at Broad Green in 1969. As is usually the case the New Inn is actually a building of considerable age, and it served buyers and dealers at the Horse Fairs on Broad Green up to the late nineteenth century. The inn closed in December 1970. The house on the right is Oak House, built on the site of another public house – the Royal Oak, whose name was taken by newly-built premises on the corner of Doddington Road and Kingsway in the late 1930s. Oak House now forms part of the Oak House Hotel. (*Lawson Pratt collection*)

High Street near the St John's Street corner around 1956. The cross on the picture marks the Post Office, which is still in the same spot. There has been little change in the buildings on this side of the street. *(John Darker)*

The opening ceremony in October 1955 of The Rotary Club of Wellingborough's shelter at Broad Green given to the then Wellingborough Urban District Council for use by senior citizens. Rotary President Chris Webb shakes hands with the Chairman of the Town Council, Albert Langham, watched by, from left to right: Rotarians Harold Cheney, Harry Battson, Dick Parker, Laurie Bolton, Harry Sursham and Ted Andrews.

War Memorial (or Cenotaph), Broad Green, built in 1924 and engraved by the Wellingborough stonemason White & Co. (*Wharton collection*)

The north-east corner of Broad Green in 1969, with the corner of Hatton Avenue just showing on the left. The first cottage, built in the typical banded ironstone of a much earlier Wellingborough, was replaced in the 1980s with a modern building. The double road junction, with Harrowden Road around to the left of Little Green, and Gold Street to the right of it, is now controlled by two sets of very necessary traffic lights, with no right turn down into High Street. (*Marjorie Veal*)

Broad Green – the front of Hatton Hall in 1970. The foundations of the house are thought to date from 1783. Amongst a number of occupants, perhaps the most notable were the Vivians – especially the Rev. Charles Pasley Vivian, who was vicar of the Parish Church from 1815 to 1841. His arms and monogram are above the porch at the front entrance. In the midst of great controversy the house was allowed to decay and was demolished, leaving only the front facade to form the facia to a block of flats built for the elderly during the early 1980s.

(*Lawson Pratt collection*)

The rear of Hatton Hall in 1970. The light colour of the lower part of the wall on the right was where a large conservatory was added before 1820. At the extreme left can be seen the low building which was the dairy. This had an octagonal shape and a Collyweston stone roof. Many townspeople will remember the Hall's one-time use at the Hatton Home for Boys, it having been acquired by the English Waifs and Strays Society in 1913. Most of the boys attended Freemans School up to and after World War II.

(*Lawson Pratt collection*)

The row of cottages which formerly stood in Westfield Road between Short Lane (with the steam-laundry chimney) and Bassetts Close (date uncertain). Facing Short Lane, off to the left, is Buckwell Green, and Short Lane runs down to the right to Buckwell End. The word 'buck' means 'to wash', and recalls the name of one of the town's ancient wells, the waters of which must have been used for the washing of clothes before steam laundry days. (*Marjorie Veal*)

The large cobbled area of Buckwell End to the left, West Street to the right and the entrance to Jacksons Lane in the centre in 1972. (*Lawson Pratt collection*)

The east side of upper West Street in 1972. The left-hand houses of the terrace can be seen in the previous photograph. All were removed during the 1980s. (*Lawson Pratt collection*)

The west side of upper West Street, looking towards Buckwell End, in 1972. The taller roof was the shop at the entrance lane to Bassetts Close. The road now runs across the site of the terrace and joins with West Villa Road.
(*Lawson Pratt collection*)

Left: Houses in Pipe Yard, off Jacksons Lane and behind West Street, in 1969. In the distance are houses in lower West Street. By this date much of Pipe Yard had already been demolished. The name came from the making of clay pipes there many years ago. This area is now part of Jacksons Lane car park.

(*Lawson Pratt collection*)

Below: Oxford Street/St Barnabas Street corner in 1970. Yorke and Company's shoe factory (previously Walkers) gave employment to about a hundred workers, mainly from the surrounding streets. There were considerable problems in the industry from the 1960s onwards because of import policies and the use of new materials for footwear. Here, demolition of the factory is under way. During the war, fire-watching duty was undertaken by a rota of employees who returned to take their watch, having worked all day in the factory. During that period most boot and shoe factories began the day at 7.30 a.m.

(*Lawson Pratt collection*)

Below: Part of the east side of Well Street in 1970. This street lay between Spring Gardens and Wood Street. Although the houses had no gardens to the street, there were quite lengthy ones at the rear. These houses are numbers 22, 24 and 26, and they give a good idea of the size of homes which were built to the regulations of the time – a frontage width of 12 ft or 15 ft was stipulated. The houses in this picture, of 12 ft width, were demolished in 1972/73.

Above: Spring Gardens, off Oxford Street, in 1968. The Spring Gardens estate was built as a western extension to the town from the 1860s when the population was rapidly expanding. Many houses had back extensions which included out-workers' shoe 'shops' or workshops. Building was mainly speculative, undertaken by a number of tradesmen, and similar townsmen, who employed builders to erect two or more cottages on their behalf. The rents then gave them an added income. Few, if any, houses of this type were built for sale, and certainly very few indeed could have afforded to buy, even though an average price at the time was between £100 and £150. The Peacock Inn, on the corner of Cross Street, was actually a rebuild of an inn of the same name in Silver Street. The terrace was demolished in the early 1970s. (*Marjorie Veal*)

The access road (known as a 'back') between Well Street (left) and Wood Street. A connecting lane ran across the far end, linking the two streets. It had no house frontages and was known locally as the Hill. In the distance is the leather works of Messrs Brown. The taller house at the end of the row was a corner shop, off-licence and general store, which ceased trading in 1953. The business was run from 1943 to 1953 by Mr A. Cyril Hadley, who was also well known in Wellingborough as an ice-cream salesman who made his own ice creams and iced lollies and sold them from a trailer behind his car.

Below: The junction of Wood Street (to the left) and Dale Street (centre) with Northampton Road, just at the point where the latter ceases to be Oxford Street, in 1968. Turnell's off-licence/store is No. 1 Northampton Road. In the distance (left) is the junction of Hill Street with Dale Street.

(Marjorie Veal)

Wood Street from Dale Street corner in 1968, with Ashby's the butchers and grocery shop. There were once no fewer than five corner shops in this single street – three of which survived until the redevelopment of the area – plus the Bantam Cock public house and off-licence. In the distance can be seen part of the new housing development which was also named Wood Street, and which some of the residents moved into. Others were housed in another new development off Northampton Road – Lea Way. (*Lawson Pratt collection*)

Wood Street looking towards Northampton Road in 1968 showing The Bantam Cock, with doors to the bar and jug-and-bottle. The white painted areas half-way up the brickwork of the doorways were relics of wartime when streets were unlit at night, and not an aid to inebriates! The premises were a conversion from two houses some time after 1895. (*Lawson Pratt collection*)

The bottom east side of Wood Street in 1975, with the leather factory, built in two stages by Brown & Son. The top floor windows of the brick building were usually open to allow natural drying of the suspended skins. Most of the area was by this time demolished, and the rough ground on the left is the site of part of South Row. The house numbered 33A, which had been amalgamated with its neighbour number 34A, was the last to be knocked down. These two house numbers give a hint to the old-style numbering of houses in the street, which ran consecutively down one side and up the other. This newer pair of houses had therefore been given 'A' numbers, and were apparently erected for factory personnel.

A closer view of the wooden addition to Brown's factory, with its overlapping glass panes to the windows and air ventilators near the apex of the roof. To the right is evidence of the new housing which had already begun to replace the old.

South Row in about 1960. This terrace of five houses faced an allotment field. Beyond the white house is the entrance to 'the Back' between Wood Street and Hill Street, and opposite this, to the left, was an unmetalled footway giving access to the allotments and entry into Croyland Road. The latter was later closed.

(*Marjorie Veal*)

Hill Street looking towards Dale Street in 1970, with some houses already vacated for demolition. (*Lawson Pratt collection*)

Dale Street from the entrance (left) to Brook Street East in 1970. In the distance is Yorke's footwear factory in Oxford Street. Only part of the terrace was scheduled for demolition – the houses nearest the camera. (*Lawson Pratt collection*)

Northampton Road from Wood Street in 1975 with the site of Ashby's butchers shop on the left. The former Congregational Chapel, seen through the trees, is now Wellingborough Workbridge.

The interior of St Barnabas Church, in St Barnabas Street, in 1949. Initially a prefabricated church, made of corrugated iron sheets, was built as a chapel-of-ease to the Parish Church in 1863. This humble structure was replaced by this church in 1893 – a dignified building of brick with dressings of Bath stone. St Barnabas had by this time become a parish in its own right, with its own vicarage. (*Lawson Pratt collection*)

My Favourite Picture

by DERYK G. WILLS

ONE evening in May, 1949, flames were seen coming from St. Barnabas' Church in Wellingborough, Northamptonshire. Soon the whole building was blazing. Deryk G. Wills, newspaper cameraman, hurried to the scene. As he was watching, a ladder bearing a fireman whose job was to direct a hose down into the fire began slowly to buckle. The fireman, realizing his danger, started to climb down as the ladder twisted under him. He finally reached the ground safely but not before Wills had captured this exciting moment. If you have taken a picture that is different, let us see it.

In 1949 on a May evening, soon after the interior picture on the left was taken, the church was found to be on fire. The blaze was caused by children setting fire to torn-up hymn books. The building became a smoking ruin. This dramatic picture appeared in the national magazine *Illustrated* on 18 November 1950 and won a national award for news cameraman Deryk Wills. A fireman trying to tackle the blaze from the eastern end of the building was very lucky to reach the ground safely after the metal ladder buckled in the great heat. (*Lawson Pratt collection*)

A 1958 aerial view of the houses between Queensway (left) and Lea Way, with Western Way in the foreground. To the left, Milton Avenue is under construction, and there were only about 26 houses completed in Shelley Road. To the right are the allotments, approached from Weavers Road (off the picture). The very large area designated as an 'overspill' area for people from London was yet to be built upon.

Another view of the area between Queensway and Lea Way in 1969, with Northampton Road in the foreground. At that time the link road between the Kingsway and Queensway estates had not been made. The start of Queensway was split into two separate two-way roads, which even confused the locals, and can still be seen in the present road pattern.

An aerial photograph looking north-east from the Queensway area in 1969. At top right is Brickhill Road, with Steele Road under construction. Brickhill Road runs along part of an ancient trackway, and at this date the section linking Brickhill houses with the Queensway estate is still unmetalled. The large building near the bottom of the picture is St Mark's Church. To the north of the trackway a large pre-Roman and Romano-British occupation site was discovered in the late 1960s. This, and the following photograph were taken as part of an aerial survey of the site made to detect cropmarks as an aid to excavation work.

A second view of the Brickhill site, with Weavers Road, the school and playing fields at top right. A number of pottery kilns were detected on the site, and some were excavated, together with a potters' workshop. The main product was coarse-ware pottery – mainly large jars for storage. Extensive evidence of a large Roman settlement was found during investigations by the Wellingborough Archaeological Society. The best of the many kilns was preserved, and its presence marked in the new road which came to be called Kiln Way by the then Urban District Council. The feature, dating from circa AD150, is still to be found today.

One of the Romano-British pottery kilns – excavated under the leadership of Mrs Gwen Brown, an archaeologist for the Ministry of Works, seen holding the measuring pole. Because of the building development, much of this large site was never excavated. (*Lawson Pratt collection*)

Brickhill Road, further up the hill and looking back to the town in 1972.

Shelley Road in 1971, with the corner of Wordsworth Road on the left, in Wellingborough's 'poets corner' estate above Queensway. The Town Development board shows two coats of arms – on the left Wellingborough Urban District Council and on the right Greater London Council, instigators of the housing developments in the town specifically for newcomers from the London area. Some of these actually knew the town well, having been evacuated to Wellingborough from the metropolis during World War II.

The same development area looking west, with Hawkshead (left) and, beyond it, Racedown under construction circa 1971.

A pleasant area with a green in Shelley Road, Queensway north, in 1974.

This picture was taken in celebration of the completion of the 1,000th home during the post-war development of the Croyland Estate. This mushroomed outwards from the earlier Kingsway Estate, and came to house many local people from the clearance areas in the town, as well as newly-weds waiting on the Council's housing list. The scene above is in Valley Road.

AERIAL VIEWS OF THE TOWN TAKEN BETWEEN 1969 and 1973

Left: The Parish Church and Technical College is on the left near the top. Doddington Road leads into the picture with the former Grammar (now Wrenn) School and the Cottage Hospital in the foreground. Croyland Hall and the Zoo Park below the Abbey is easily discernible, as is the large car park laid out over the former brewery site near the Lyric cinema.

Above: The Croyland Estate, with Berrymoor Road running diagonally across the picture and into Jubilee Crescent at top right, with the shops and flats half-way along it. Kingsway runs along the upper part of the view, with Croyland Park beyond it. This was the area of the post-war housing boom in local council houses, a number of which were concrete prefabricated houses known as 'Orlit'. All of the latter have now been cleared, and the block of shops and flats is under a demolition order.

Here, the Congregational (now United Reformed) Church is on the far left, and West Street runs from the bottom left down to Oxford Street.
There are several 'yards' of houses on what is now Jacksons Lane car park (lower left).
The Tithe Barn overlooks a grassy area with many trees – now Sharman Road car park.

Broad Green from the north, with Hatton Street (left) and Debdale Road running towards the Green. Hatton Hall is not yet demolished. Except for the facade it has now gone forever, and has been replaced by flats for the elderly.

Park Road runs like an arrow into Gloucester Place (left). In Park Road the large building was erected as a one-floor shoe factory by Sudborough & Wood. Later this became 'the Mica' (or Copeland and Jenkins) and afterwards Potters DIY and furniture store. This was the scene of a fire in 1989 and the business did not reopen. Near the centre at the bottom of the picture are Box Gardens and Holly Gardens between Park Road and George Street (now both gone).

Above: The town centre. Close study shows many features now gone or considerably changed. The old Technical Institute building has just been removed – leaving only brick rubble – near the new College in Church Street which, together with the Queen Street workshops area, dominates the picture. There is, as yet, no entrance from Church Street to the Market Street area (Orient Way) and Orient House can still be seen facing the churchyard to the right of the church. Church Way is still full of buildings that run up to Orient House. Buildings on the left of Market Hill are still standing, and the area at and behind the Pebble Lane Library and shops site is a car park. But Fine Fare supermarket has replaced the familiar landmark of the Regal cinema.

Right: Not an aerial photograph, but taken from the new Technical College building. The new building dominating the scene beyond the church is the new Post Office telephone exchange in Midland Road.

Overlooking the Parish Hall of All Hallows, the area east of Silver Street can be seen, together with the Market Square buildings, now removed and replaced by the modern bank and Woolworth buildings.

From the College building we can see (centre-left) the Tithe Barn in an unrenovated state. The building which appears to be just in front of it is the old Silver cinema in Silver Street. Centre-right is Freemans Endowed School, and bottom-left is the site of the yet-to-be-built Orient Way.

Bassetts Close, with Westfield Road in the foreground. Beyond the bandstand a fun-fair is in operation. At the top is the Spring Gardens Estate running right to the large transport depot in Croyland Road. This area became entirely rebuilt with houses and flats – some new housing already having been built at the top left (Monks Way development). At centre left is Buckwell End and the open square in West Street, and Pipe Yard is on the edge of the picture off Jacksons Lane. In the lower right corner is the entrance to Brickhill Road.

The view into the town from Cannon Street, with Great Park Street in the foreground. Parts of Bell Street and Furnace Street (off Cannon Street) have been demolished. At the top of the picture the cattle market in Castle Road is still set up with animal enclosures.

A fine low level aerial view around 1964 of the north end of the town, with Hatton Hall lower left and Buckwell End right. On the far left can be seen the undeveloped area used before World War II as the fairground. This was behind the United Counties bus garage in St John Street. (*Lawson Pratt collection*)

A 1946 picture taken by Vic Baines from the Church spire. In the foreground left are the remains of White Horse Yard, whilst to the right is the back of Barclays Bank and Woolworths. The large building just left of centre is the Lyric cinema. The patchwork appearance of its roof results from repairs to damage caused by a wartime bomb across the road in the Post Office yard. The chimney marks the brewery premises of Campbell Praed & Co. Ltd. (*Collection of Mrs E. Pettitt*)

This is the first of a series of photos from the Lawson Pratt collection taken over a period of a few weeks in March 1974 from various positions on top of the new Post Office building. They form a complete circle of view taken just before the demolitions prior to the building of the new shopping precinct. This is Midland Road looking over the Police Station to the Castle Street area.

The former Lyric, by this time a bingo hall. Beyond is the large car park covering the site of the old brewery.

Moving to the right, the Lyric again, and beyond the Castle Road and London Road area, with on the left the large store built in the former cattle market, then Brierley's supermarket.

The old Lyric cinema building with, on the extreme right, the old Tudor houses in Sheep Street. Near the top of the view is the sweep of Doddington Road, with Swanspool Gardens to the left.

Now looking almost due west. In the foreground are the old offices of the Gas Company (with the car parked outside), and in the middle distance can be seen the girders for the new Beeswing House under construction in Sheep Street. Top right the new insurance offices in Tithe Barn Road near completion.

The top of Midland Road. On the left the cottages in Cheese Lane are already being stripped. The flat-topped building in the middle is the office block of the WICS. By the time this photograph was taken all the shops in Midland Road had closed down.

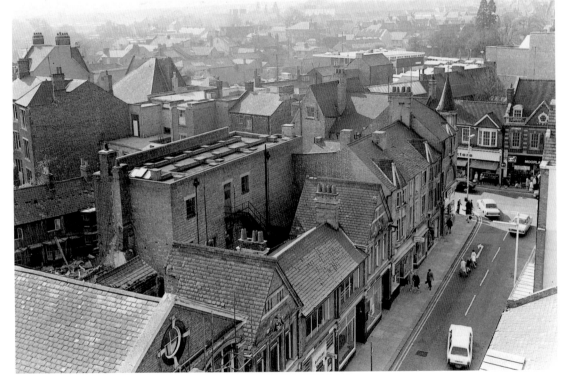

The top of Midland Road and the rear of Market Street. The back of the new Library is visible below the Technical College and Church.

The view now includes the back of Church Street in the distance, with the vicarage and church yard.

The foreground shows the back of Market Street and Cambridge Street, with the passage next to the public house on the extreme right. In the centre is the Palace cinema, and to the right are the buildings of Park Road.

The rear of Cambridge Street with old 'Mathers Yard' in the centre leading down to the remains of Wellingborough's second tithe barn – the ironstone banded building with pantiled roof was part of Hatton Manor originally.

The factories behind Cambridge Street.
The Chequers Inn is on the left of the picture.

Dominating this view is the former factory and chimney of the Ideal Clothiers.
On the skyline is the distinctive tower of Victoria School
and on the right is St Mary's Church.

Moving further to the right of the Ideal factory towards the back of the east side of
Midland Road. The house (bottom right) is in Glen Bank.

Now we are back to Midland Road looking south – completing the circuit.

Wilby Lido around 1950. Other than the river, this was the only bathing place for the Wellingborough area, and a frequent cycle trip for schoolchildren in the summer months. The site was formerly a brickyard and claypit.

The Wilby Lido on Tuesday 2 August 1960 – a happy scene during a Bank Holiday week.
The local schools also used this pool for swimming classes. (*Northampton Chronicle & Echo*)

Wilby Lido at the same time as the previous picture was taken. Who were these young ladies? (*Northampton Chronicle & Echo*)

Hardwater Crossing on the former railway line along the Nene valley to Northampton. The barrier and warning lights replaced a single gate crossing. The line closed to all passenger traffic in 1964.

Below: The Hardwater Crossing signal box which faced the lines on the Great Doddington side of the double tracks. (*Bob Hill*)

Rushden Station on Tuesday 17 March 1959, with 300 children waiting for the train to Wellingborough on their way to see Rev. Brian Hession's film on the life of Christ called *Day of Triumph*.(*Northampton Chronicle & Echo*)

INDEX

aerial views 169-70, 174-7, 179-80
Angel Hotel 108, 114
Attlee, Clement 9

Bassetts Close 179
Berrymoor Road 174
boots and shoes 124-5, 161
breaker's yard 140
breweries 62, 68, 69, 78, 81, 119, 182
Brickhill Road 170-1
bridges 123, 127, 130, 145
Broad Green 155-8
Buckwell End 159
Burystead Place 100, 102-3, 106

Cambridge Street 57-9, 61, 185, 186
Cannon Street 56, 154, 179
carnivals 47, 51
Cattle Market 53-4
Cheese Lane 48, 75, 79, 80
Church Way 115
churches:
  All Hallows 23, 118
  All Saints 67
  Congregational Chapel 167
  St Barnabas 168
  St Mark's 170
  St Mary's 186
  United Reformed 175
churchyard 118, 178
cinemas:
  Regal 8, 9, 12, 13
  Lyric 38, 40, 42, 45, 48, 50, 70, 78,
    182, 183
  Palace 60, 185
  Silver Cinema 178
College 11
Commercial Lane 74, 77, 78
Cross Road 148
Cross Street 162
Croyland Abbey 87, 91-2, 98, 103

Dale Street 163, 167

Denington Estate 124-5
Dulley's baths 55

factories 122-4, 128, 149, 165, 186
Finedon Road 136, 138, 147
fires 107, 168
foundry 136, 144
funfair 179

Glen Bank 186
Gloucester Place 37
Gold Street 150-1
Grammar School, The old 118

Hardwater Crossing 190
Hatton Hall 158, 176, 180
Havelock Street 6
Hawkshead 172
Hemmingwell Estate 147
High Street 116, 156
Hill Street 166
Hind Hotel rear endpaper, 24, 25, 34,
  68, 71, 73, 100, 105

Iron works 137-8
Irthlingborough Road 136, 139

Jackson's Lane 159

Kiln Way 170-1

Lea Way 169
Leighton House 115
library 16, 20
Lindgren, George 9
Little Irchester 131
Little Park Street 153
London Road 81, 119, 121, 131

market 17, 20
Market Square 12-13, 72, endpapers
Market Street 21, 22, 25-9, 31-7, 48,
  110-11, 185

Midland Road 30, 38-47, 49-52, 183-6
mills 123, 126-8
Milton Avenue 169
Motor cycle training scheme 54

narrow boat 128
New Street 149
newspaper offices 63
Northampton Road 167

Orchard Terrace 155

Pagoda 8, 13, 24
Park Road 60, 176
Pebble Lane 19, 23
Pipe Yard 161
Pendered's 16, 19
Public houses:
  Angel Hotel 108, 112, 114
  Bantam Cock 164
  Bee's Wing 67, 69
  Cambridge Hotel 57
  Chequers 59, 186
  Crown 24, 34
  Crown & Anchor 130
  Dewdrop 59
  Exchange Hotel 10, 14, 16, 18
  Globe 37
  Golden Lion 62, 65
  New Inn 155
  Old King's Arms 31
  Peacock 162
  Rising Sun 59
  Swan & Nest 154
Pyghtle, The 148

Queen Street 154
Queensway 169

Racedown 172
railways: Hardwater Crossing 190
  ironstone 136
  London Road station 129, 131-4

Midland Road station 141, 143-4,
  146
Rushden station 191
  traffic 135, 139, 142-6
Regent Street 152
River Nene 122, 127, 130
Rushden 191

St Barnabas Street 161, 168
St John's Street 149
Salvation Army 24
schools 112, 118, 119, 148, 174, 178
Sheep Street 10-11, 62-7, 69, 71, 73,
  76, 83-5, 98
Shelley Road 169, 172, 173
shopping centre 79, 81
Short Lane 159
Silver Street 18, 108-9, 112-15
South Row 166
Spring Gardens 162
Swanspool frontispiece, 117, 119-20
Swanspool Brook 89, 99
sweep 6

Tithe Barn 82, 101, 104, 106, 107, 185
Town Hall 112

Valley Road 173

War Memorial 157,
Well Street 162, 163
West Street 160
Western Way 169
Westfield Road 159
White Horse Yard 182
White Place 14, 15, 19
Whitworth family 105
Wilby Lido 187-9
Wood Street 163-5
Woolworth's 14
Wordsworth Road 172

Zoo Park 84-90, 93-7